THE ULTIMATE HAIR BRAIDI

Step-By-Step Instructions For Box Braids, Cornrows, French, Dutch, Lemonade, And More – For All Hair Types And Textures

Richard P. Hutson

Table of Contents

Chapter 1: Introduction to Hair Braiding.....4

   What Is Hair Braiding? 4

Chapter 2: Tools and Materials Needed......6

   Essential Tools for Braiding......................6

Chapter 3: Preparing Hair for Braiding 8

   Washing and Detangling 8

Chapter 4: Basic Braiding Techniques 10

   Three-Strand Braid 10

Chapter 5: Advanced Braiding Styles.........12

Chapter 6: Step-by-Step Guide to Box Braids 14

   Sectioning Hair for Box Braids 14

Chapter 7: Creating Cornrows with Precision 16

   Planning Your Design 16

Chapter 8: Mastering French and Dutch Braids..18

Differences Between French and Dutch Braids 18

Chapter 9: Styling and Decorating Braids ..20

Adding Beads and Accessories...............20

Chapter 10: Braiding for All Hair Lengths ..22

Working with Short Hair 22

Chapter 11: Maintenance and Care for Braids..24

Chapter 12: Troubleshooting Common Braiding Challenges 26

Chapter 13: Creative Braiding Ideas and Inspiration 28

Trendy Braids to Try..............................28

THE END...36

Chapter 1: Introduction to Hair Braiding

What Is Hair Braiding?

Hair braiding is the art of weaving three or more strands of hair together to create various styles and patterns. This technique allows hair to be styled in ways that are both beautiful and functional. Braids can range from simple, everyday styles to intricate designs that showcase creativity and skill. They can be worn by people with all hair types and textures, offering versatility and endless possibilities.

Brief History and Cultural Significance

Braiding has a rich and diverse history, with roots tracing back thousands of years across many cultures worldwide. From ancient African tribes to Native American communities, braids have served not only as a form of personal expression but also as symbols of identity, social status, and heritage. Over time, braiding evolved into an art form celebrated in fashion and culture globally. Today, braids continue to connect people to their history while inspiring new trends and styles.

Benefits of Braiding for All Hair Types

Braiding offers several advantages that make it a popular choice for hairstyling. It helps keep hair neat and tidy, making it easier to manage throughout the day. Braids can protect hair from daily wear and tear, while also allowing individuals to experiment with various looks without heat or chemicals. Suitable for all hair types, braiding is a versatile option that adapts to different textures and lengths, providing creative freedom and style longevity.

Chapter 2: Tools and Materials Needed

Essential Tools for Braiding

Having the right tools makes the braiding process smoother and helps achieve neat, professional-looking results. Basic tools include a wide-tooth comb for detangling hair gently, a rat-tail comb for precise parting, and hair clips or sectioning clips to hold hair in place during styling. You'll also want hair elastics or bands to secure the ends of braids, and a spray bottle filled with water to keep hair manageable throughout the process.

Selecting Hair Extensions and Accessories

Extensions can add length, volume, or color to your braids, allowing for more creative styles. When choosing hair extensions, consider synthetic or natural options based on your preference and the desired look. It's important to select extensions that blend well with your natural hair texture for a seamless finish. Additionally, accessories like beads, cuffs, and ribbons can personalize and enhance your braids, adding flair and uniqueness.

Preparing Your Workspace

A clean, well-lit workspace helps you focus and keeps the braiding process organized. Choose a comfortable chair and set up a mirror at eye level to see your work clearly. Arrange all tools and materials within easy reach to avoid interruptions. Keeping a towel or cape handy can help protect your clothes from stray hair or products. Creating a dedicated space for braiding can make the experience more enjoyable and efficient.

Chapter 3: Preparing Hair for Braiding

Washing and Detangling

Before braiding, it's important to start with clean hair. Washing removes dirt, oils, and buildup, creating a fresh foundation for styling. After washing, gently detangle hair using a wide-tooth comb or fingers, starting from the ends and working upward toward the roots. This careful approach prevents breakage and makes braiding easier and smoother. Clean and detangled hair helps the braid hold better and appear neat.

Sectioning Techniques

Proper sectioning is key to creating uniform and well-organized braids. Use a rat-tail comb to divide hair into manageable sections based on the braid style you plan to create. For styles like box braids, square or rectangular sections work best, while cornrows may require long, narrow sections following the scalp's shape. Secure sections with clips or hair ties to keep them separated as you work. Clear sectioning saves time and leads to a more polished final look.

Choosing the Right Products (Non-Medical)

Selecting suitable hair products can enhance the braiding experience without making any medical claims. Lightweight leave-in conditioners, styling creams, or natural oils help improve manageability and add shine. Avoid heavy or greasy products that may weigh hair down or make it slippery. Using a light mist of water can also help maintain moisture during braiding. These products support smooth handling and help the style last longer while keeping the hair looking vibrant.

Chapter 4: Basic Braiding Techniques

Three-Strand Braid

The three-strand braid is the foundation of most braiding styles. It involves dividing the hair into three equal sections and crossing them over one another in a simple, repeating pattern. Starting by crossing the right section over the middle, then the left section over the middle, you continue alternating until the braid reaches the desired length. This technique is easy to learn and creates a classic, timeless look suitable for all hair types.

French Braid Basics

The French braid adds elegance and complexity to the basic three-strand braid by gradually incorporating hair from the scalp as you braid. Begin by gathering a small section of hair at the crown and dividing it into three parts. As you braid downwards, add small sections of hair from the sides into each strand before crossing it over the middle. This method produces a braid that lies flat against the head, making it both stylish and secure.

Dutch Braid Basics

The Dutch braid, sometimes called the inverted or inside-out braid, is similar to the French braid but with a different weaving technique. Instead of crossing the strands over the middle section, you cross them underneath. This creates a braid that appears raised or "popped out" from the scalp. Like the French braid, hair is added gradually as you move down, giving the style a bold and textured appearance.

Chapter 5: Advanced Braiding Styles

Box Braids

Box braids are a popular protective style featuring individual braids sectioned into small square-shaped parts, resembling boxes. This style offers versatility, allowing braids of varying lengths and thicknesses. Box braids can be worn naturally or accessorized with beads and cuffs for a personalized look. They are suitable for all hair types and textures, providing a stylish and manageable option.

Cornrows

Cornrows are braids woven close to the scalp in straight or curved lines, creating geometric patterns or designs. This style is known for its neat appearance and durability. Cornrows can be simple or intricate, depending on the pattern chosen. They can also serve as a base for adding extensions or combining with other styles, offering both aesthetic appeal and practicality.

Lemonade Braids

Named after a popular cultural reference, lemonade braids are a variation of cornrows styled primarily to one side of the head. They create a sleek, asymmetrical look that is both trendy and elegant. Lemonade braids can vary in thickness and pattern complexity, making them adaptable for different occasions and personal styles.

Chapter 6: Step-by-Step Guide to Box Braids

Sectioning Hair for Box Braids

Start by thoroughly detangling the hair to ensure smooth braiding. Use a rat-tail comb to divide the hair into small, even square sections. The size of each section will determine the thickness of the braids, so choose according to your preference. Secure each section with clips or small hair ties to keep them separate and organized throughout the process. Taking time with neat sectioning sets the foundation for clean and uniform braids.

Braiding Method

For each section, divide the hair into three equal strands. Begin braiding by crossing the strands over each other, continuing the three-strand braid technique down the length of the hair. If you are adding extensions, place them at the root and braid them together with the natural hair for added length and volume. Maintain consistent tension as you braid to ensure the braid is secure but comfortable. Repeat this process for every section until the entire head is braided.

Finishing Touches

Once all braids are complete, trim any stray hairs for a polished appearance. You can dip the ends of synthetic braids in warm water to seal them and prevent unraveling. Adding accessories such as beads or cuffs can personalize your style. Finally, gently style the edges or baby hairs with a lightweight gel or styling cream to frame the face. These finishing steps help the box braids look neat, lasting, and fashionable.

Chapter 7: Creating Cornrows with Precision

Planning Your Design

Before starting cornrows, take a moment to plan the design you want to create. Cornrows can be simple straight lines, curved patterns, or intricate shapes. Using a mirror, map out the sections on your scalp with a comb or parting tool. You can draw inspiration from pictures or customize your own unique style. Clear planning helps ensure your cornrows look balanced and well-organized.

Braiding Tight and Loose Cornrows

Cornrows can be braided with varying tension depending on your preference. Tight cornrows create a sleek, defined look and last longer, while looser cornrows offer a softer, more comfortable style. Start by sectioning a small area close to the scalp, then divide it into three strands. Begin braiding by crossing the outer strands under the middle one, adding hair as you move forward along the scalp. Keep your hand movements steady and consistent to maintain even tension.

Adding Extensions (If Desired)

Extensions can be added to cornrows for extra length, thickness, or color variation. To add extensions, select synthetic or natural hair that matches your desired look. Start by placing the extension hair at the root alongside your natural hair, then braid them together. Be careful to keep the tension comfortable to avoid strain. Adding extensions can enhance the style's versatility and create a more dramatic effect.

Chapter 8: Mastering French and Dutch Braids

Differences Between French and Dutch Braids

While both French and Dutch braids involve weaving hair close to the scalp, the main difference lies in the weaving technique. French braids are created by crossing the strands over the middle section, resulting in a braid that lies flat against the head. Dutch braids, on the other hand, cross the strands under the middle section, making the braid appear raised or "inside out." Understanding this difference helps you choose the style that best fits your desired look.

Techniques for Clean, Neat Braids

To achieve clean and neat braids, start with detangled hair and clear sectioning. Use a rat-tail comb to part hair evenly, and work with manageable sections. Keep consistent tension as you braid, avoiding too tight or too loose strands. Smooth hair with your fingers or a light styling product to reduce flyaways. Taking your time and working carefully ensures polished, professional results.

Styling Ideas

French and Dutch braids are versatile and can be worn in many ways. Try a single braid down the back for a classic look, or create two braids for a sporty, youthful style. Combining braids into buns, ponytails, or updos adds variety and elegance. These braids also pair well with accessories like ribbons, beads, or hair cuffs for a personalized touch.

Chapter 9: Styling and Decorating Braids

Adding Beads and Accessories

Beads, cuffs, and other hair accessories can enhance the look of your braids, adding personality and flair. Choose accessories that complement your style and hair color. Beads can be threaded onto individual braids or added at the ends for a decorative finish. Hair cuffs and rings can be clipped around braids at various points to create eye-catching details. Accessories offer a simple way to customize your braids and make them stand out.

Wrapping and Styling Braids

Wrapping braids with colorful threads or ribbons adds texture and vibrancy to your style. Wrap the material tightly but gently around sections of braid, securing the ends discreetly. Braids can also be styled into updos, ponytails, buns, or half-up styles for different occasions. Experimenting with wrapping and styling helps you refresh your look without needing a full redo.

Transitioning Braids into Other Hairstyles

Braids are versatile and can be integrated into other hairstyles. For example, braided sections can be combined with loose hair to create boho-chic waves, or incorporated into ponytails and buns for elegant or casual looks. Using braids as accents or base structures allows for creativity and variation, making your hairstyle adaptable to any event or mood.

Chapter 10: Braiding for All Hair Lengths

Working with Short Hair

Braiding short hair can be both creative and stylish. Smaller, tighter braids or cornrows work well with shorter lengths, offering neatness and versatility. Using texturizing sprays or light styling creams can help add grip and control during braiding. Patience and gentle handling are key to achieving clean braids without tugging.

Medium-Length Hair Braiding Tips

Medium-length hair offers more flexibility with braiding styles. You can experiment with classic braids, French or Dutch braids, and even start incorporating extensions if desired. Sectioning becomes important for neatness, and using clips can help keep hair organized while working. Medium lengths provide a balance of manageability and style options.

Long Hair Braiding Techniques

Long hair allows for the most intricate and voluminous braids. When working with longer hair, ensure thorough detangling to avoid knots. Consider braiding in sections to manage the hair's weight and length. Styles like box braids or multiple cornrows work beautifully with long hair, and adding accessories can enhance the overall look. Taking breaks during the braiding process helps maintain comfort and precision.

Chapter 11: Maintenance and Care for Braids

Daily Care Tips

Keeping your braids looking fresh starts with simple daily habits. Gently moisturizing your scalp and braids with light sprays or oils helps maintain softness and shine. Avoid heavy products that may cause buildup. Use a soft brush or your fingers to smooth down any flyaways and keep edges tidy. Regularly checking your braids for loose strands ensures they stay neat longer.

Nighttime Protection Techniques

Protecting braids while you sleep helps maintain their neatness. Use a satin or silk scarf, bonnet, or pillowcase to reduce friction and prevent frizz. You can also gently wrap your braids or tie them up to avoid tangling overnight. These simple steps help extend the life of your braids and keep them looking polished.

When to Remove Braids

Braids should be removed when they start to loosen significantly or when your scalp feels uncomfortable. Typically, styles like box braids or cornrows can be kept for several weeks, but it's important not to keep them in too long. Removing braids in a timely manner allows your hair to rest and prepare for the next style.

Chapter 12: Troubleshooting Common Braiding Challenges

Managing Frizz

Frizz can appear during or after braiding, especially with natural or textured hair. To manage frizz, start with well-moisturized and detangled hair. Using a light styling cream or gel can help smooth flyaways during braiding. After braiding, applying a light mist or oil can keep the hair looking polished. Avoid over-manipulating braids to maintain their neat appearance.

Handling Uneven Sections

Uneven sections can affect the symmetry and overall look of your braids. Use a fine-tooth comb or rat-tail comb to create clean, precise parts before braiding. If a section is too large or small, adjust it early in the process to keep braids balanced. Taking your time during sectioning reduces the chances of uneven braids.

Avoiding Breakage

Preventing breakage is important for maintaining healthy hair while braiding. Work gently to avoid pulling or tugging on hair strands. Use adequate but comfortable tension when braiding to keep styles secure without strain. Regularly moisturizing hair before braiding adds flexibility, making it easier to braid without stress on the strands.

Chapter 13: Creative Braiding Ideas and Inspiration

Trendy Braids to Try

Explore the latest braid trends to keep your style fresh and fashionable. Styles like waterfall braids, halo braids, and fishtail braids offer unique looks that can be adapted for daily wear or special events. Experimenting with different braid sizes and patterns lets you create a look that's modern and eye-catching.

Braids for Special Occasions

Braids can be styled elegantly for weddings, parties, and other celebrations. Combining braids with curls, updos, or accessories elevates your hairstyle for formal events. Consider braided crowns, braided buns, or intricate braided patterns to complement your outfit and personal style.

Customizing Braids for Personal Style

Make your braids uniquely yours by incorporating colors, beads, and creative parting patterns. Mixing braiding techniques in one style adds dimension and interest. Personal touches allow your hairstyle to reflect your personality and mood, making braiding not just a skill but an art form.

Conclusion: Embracing the Art of Hair Braiding

Hair braiding is much more than a styling technique—it is a timeless form of self-expression, creativity, and cultural heritage that has evolved across generations and geographies. From simple three-strand braids to complex cornrows and box braids, this handbook has aimed to guide you through the vast world of braiding with clarity, precision, and inspiration.

Throughout the chapters, you have discovered the foundational knowledge and practical skills necessary to master braiding for all hair types and textures. We began by understanding what hair braiding truly is, appreciating its rich history and cultural significance around the world. Recognizing this context adds deeper meaning to every braid you create and wear, turning each style into a celebration of tradition and artistry.

Getting started with the right tools and materials sets the stage for success. Choosing the essential combs, brushes, and hair accessories helps streamline your braiding process and achieves professional-looking results. Preparing your workspace and hair properly ensures a smooth and enjoyable experience, making every session efficient and focused.

Understanding your unique hair type and texture is vital. Adapting braiding techniques to suit curly, wavy, coily, or straight hair ensures the best results while honoring the natural characteristics of your hair. Preparation steps such as washing, detangling, and sectioning create a solid base for neat, durable braids. Knowing which non-medical products work best for your hair texture helps maintain softness and manageability without overloading the hair.

We explored the basic braiding techniques— three-strand, French, and Dutch braids—which form the foundation for more advanced styles. Mastering these essential braids gives you confidence to experiment with complex looks like box braids, cornrows, and lemonade braids. Each style comes with its own flair and versatility, offering endless opportunities for creativity.

The step-by-step guides provided clear instructions to perfect each braiding style. From sectioning hair meticulously to executing the braid with consistent tension and finishing with neat edges or accessories, every detail was highlighted. These practical tips are designed to help both beginners and those refining their skills achieve salon-quality results at home.

Styling and decorating braids unlock a world of personalization. Adding beads, cuffs, or colorful threads transforms basic braids into stunning statements. Wrapping techniques and versatile styling options—like updos or ponytails—offer dynamic looks suited for any occasion, from casual outings to special celebrations. Braids are not just protective hairstyles; they are a canvas for self-expression.

We also addressed braiding for all hair lengths, demonstrating how short, medium, and long hair each present unique challenges and advantages. With the right techniques, all hair lengths can be braided beautifully, ensuring no one is left out of this art form.

Maintenance and care are essential to prolonging the life and beauty of your braids. Simple daily habits and nighttime protection help keep braids fresh and neat, while timely removal prevents unnecessary strain on the hair. These practical suggestions support a balanced approach that respects the hair's integrity while enjoying the style.

Troubleshooting common challenges like frizz, uneven sections, and potential breakage provides realistic solutions to common hurdles. By working patiently and gently, you can avoid frustration and ensure your braids remain tidy and comfortable.

Finally, creative braiding ideas encourage you to push the boundaries of traditional styles. Trendy braids, special occasion looks, and customization inspire continuous innovation. Your braids can reflect your personality and mood, transforming hair braiding into a personal art form that grows with you.

By mastering the skills in this handbook, you now hold the power to create diverse and beautiful braided hairstyles with confidence. Remember, practice is key. Each braid you create strengthens your technique and deepens your appreciation for this versatile craft.

Braiding connects us to a legacy shared by countless cultures worldwide. It's a form of storytelling, identity, and creativity rolled into one. As you continue to explore and develop your braiding skills, let each strand woven be a thread in your own unique story.

Thank you for embarking on this journey with **"THE ULTIMATE HAIR BRAIDING HANDBOOK."** May it inspire your creativity and become a trusted companion in your hairstyling adventures for years to come.

THE END